# VOICINGS

# Voicings

## Carroll Blair

Aveon Publishing Company

Copyright © 2012 by Carroll Blair

All rights reserved. No part of this book may be reproduced, or transmitted in any form or by any means, electronic or mechanical, including photocopy, recording, or by any information storage and retrieval system without prior permission of the publisher.

ISBN: 978-1-936430-21-5

Library of Congress Control Number
2012948128

Aveon Publishing Co.
P.O. Box 380739
Cambridge, MA 02238-0739 USA

Also by Carroll Blair

*Grains of Thought*
*Facing the Circle*
*Reel to Real*
*Shifting Tides*
*Reaches*
*Out of Silence*
*Quarter Notes*
*By Rays of Light*
*Into the Inner Life*
*Gnosis of the Heart*
*Soul Reflections*
*Beneath and Beyond the Surface*
*Of Courage and Commitment*
*For Today and Tomorrow*
*In Meditation*
*Sightings Along the Journey*
*Through Desert's Fire*
*Offerings to Pilgrims*
*Human Natures*
*(Of Animal and Spiritual)*
*Atoms from the Suns of Solitude*
*Colors of Devotion*

# Contents

## Part I

| | |
|---|---|
| From the Nectar of the Muse | 1 |
| Never Completely Alone | 2 |
| Emeralds of the Heart | 2 |
| Clad High | 3 |
| In Some Ways | 3 |
| Closing on a Maze | 4 |
| Every Life | 4 |
| Alphabets | 5 |
| Change but Never Changing | 5 |
| Light | 6 |
| Forever Open | 6 |
| The Cutting Edge | 7 |
| Wanting Without | 7 |
| As the Story Goes | 8 |
| Caught in a Day's Delight | 8 |
| Stillness | 9 |
| By Glass Cages | 9 |
| A Coming | 10 |
| Eternal Pregnancy | 10 |
| From a Spiritual Shore | 11 |
| Hands & Knees | 11 |
| Before Its Demise | 12 |

| | |
|---|---|
| Life's Song | 12 |
| Tools | 13 |
| Rusting Faithfully | 14 |
| Clinging to the Wall of Beat | 14 |
| Always a Place | 15 |
| Going On | 15 |
| A Step or Two | 16 |
| The Noble Aim | 16 |
| First Wisdom | 17 |
| Two Egos | 17 |
| Trouble Spots | 18 |
| Loser's Revenge | 18 |
| Yes, But | 19 |
| Crowded House | 19 |
| Chipping Away | 20 |
| Abrupt Formations | 20 |
| Bending a Wave | 21 |
| For the Rose to the Rose | 21 |
| Just a Theory | 22 |
| The Object of Objectivity | 23 |
| In Life's Journey | 23 |
| To Join the Fantasy | 24 |
| Truth Colored Glasses | 24 |
| Snake Eyes | 25 |
| Waiting for the Mind's Sun | 26 |
| No Forwarding Address | 27 |
| Pages | 28 |

| | |
|---|---|
| To the Artist in Search of a Direction | 28 |
| Not a Guess | 29 |
| Most Valuable Gems | 29 |
| Sentenced to Life | 30 |
| Always the Case | 30 |
| For a Time | 31 |
| Sometimes Killing | 31 |
| Nature's Ghost | 32 |
| Dream Play | 32 |
| A World Impervious | 33 |
| Of Matinees Only | 34 |
| As Time Rushes On | 35 |
| Of Smile and Frown | 35 |
| In the Safest Place | 36 |
| As Far as the Eye Can See | 36 |
| Somewhere | 37 |
| Lying Bare | 37 |
| Beyond Life's Dream | 38 |
| Must It Be | 39 |
| Not Yet Ready | 40 |
| Question | 40 |
| With Rare Exception | 41 |
| World of Ego | 41 |
| Of Paying Attention | 42 |
| Power's Secret | 43 |
| A Dangerous Thing | 43 |
| Climbing the Walls (spiritually speaking) | 44 |
| Masked Ball Without the Dance | 44 |

| | |
|---|---|
| Life Lite | 45 |
| In the Human World | 45 |
| Crossing In and Out | 46 |
| An Artist Must Stay on His Toes . . . | 47 |
| Not Always on Time | 47 |
| Solitary Line | 48 |
| To a Suicide Friend | 49 |
| Poems | 49 |
| Solitude Shared by Two | 50 |
| Between Eyes | 50 |
| With and Without | 51 |
| The Highest Love | 51 |
| Truth at All Cost | 52 |
| By Grace to Dust | 52 |
| Place of Heed | 53 |
| Paradox Indispensable | 53 |
| More Slowly in the Depths | 54 |
| The Way of Good Fortune | 55 |
| Sometimes Better from the Shore | 55 |
| On a Rising | 56 |
| Always Speaking | 57 |
| Of Newborn Life | 57 |
| A Child's Exploration | 58 |
| Never More Giving | 58 |
| On Standing the Heat | 59 |
| Doing What They Must | 60 |
| Up to You | 61 |
| The Poet's Business | 62 |

# Part II

| | |
|---|---:|
| First Page | 65 |
| A Field | 66 |
| Ephemeral Portrait | 67 |
| A Toss of Reverence | 67 |
| In Metaplay Only | 68 |
| Places Privileged | 69 |
| Holding a Balance | 70 |
| Wound Up | 70 |
| A Mutt Called Freedom | 71 |
| How Much Is Seen | 72 |
| Lives | 72 |
| Reaching Boldly | 73 |
| Political Battles | 73 |
| Poets & Madmen | 74 |
| What Can He Tell Us | 75 |
| May It Be Asked | 76 |
| Sunday Then Monday | 76 |
| Not Ringing True | 77 |
| In the Details Only | 78 |
| How Many Missed | 78 |
| Paradox | 79 |
| Reminder | 79 |
| In Offering | 80 |
| Within Pain | 81 |
| What Remains | 81 |
| Should Always Be One | 82 |

| | |
|---|---:|
| Even in Paradise | 83 |
| Of the Genius of Nature | 83 |
| Fills with Wonder | 84 |
| Realized in a Moment | 85 |
| Time | 86 |
| What Death and the Highest Things in Life Have in Common . . . | 86 |
| A Cool Start | 87 |
| Found Mentor | 87 |
| Like a Great Athlete Never Used | 88 |
| Bending but Not Yielding | 89 |
| Grand Enough | 90 |
| Never to Be Known | 90 |
| Lost Promise | 91 |
| Not for Everyone | 91 |
| Preservation | 92 |
| Cover of Surprise | 93 |
| In Vision | 94 |
| Imprisoned Fantasies | 95 |
| No One Noticed | 96 |
| To the Dogs | 97 |
| Fault Lines | 98 |
| 10, 20, 30% Off . . . | 99 |
| Comfort Killers | 99 |
| Bourgeois Paranoia | 100 |
| Balloons in the Air | 100 |
| Pressing Buttons | 101 |

| | |
|---|---|
| Wanting | 102 |
| Modern Deficit | 103 |
| Walking in Their Sleep | 104 |
| Easy Entry | 104 |
| What Price | 105 |
| How Many Swamplands | 106 |
| Like Rare Flowers | 106 |
| My Oh My | 107 |
| Never Without Beauty | 108 |
| More Vast Than the Distance Between the Stars | 109 |
| Amidst the Gray Shadow | 109 |
| Life Needs Its Prayer | 110 |
| Images | 110 |
| Perhaps | 111 |
| Dream of a Dream | 111 |
| A Twilight | 112 |
| One Day Open | 113 |
| To the Edge | 114 |
| Stirred to Life | 115 |
| Whole in Peace | 116 |
| Covered Ground | 117 |
| Cost What It May | 117 |
| More in Common Than This | 118 |
| What Sometimes Happens | 118 |
| Song That Won't Be Sung | 119 |
| Rare the Life | 120 |
| Tears and Pain | 120 |
| Everywhere the Heart Goes | 121 |

| | |
|---|---:|
| Meaning | 122 |
| Can See Magic | 123 |
| Serenity of Love | 124 |
| Your Way | 124 |
| Thoughts | 125 |
| Words of the Soul — To the Soul | 126 |
| No Greater Benefit | 127 |
| Every Moment of One's Life | 128 |
| Keeping On | 129 |
| Who Lift Their Eyes | 130 |

# Part One

## From the Nectar of the Muse

A sip from the nectar of the muse . . .
ahhh, something to wet the lips of a
dry spell, moisten the soil of possibility
(yes) a promising thing, a profound gift
from the invisible power of the shadows
that grants to man his most powerful light

## Never Completely Alone

In tuned authority crickets chirp their songs
through the cool of the night, reminding one that
aloneness is never complete — that the hours pass
through darkness and light with abundant life
pulsating all around you, heard and unheard,
seen and unseen; that no one is ever
completely      alone




## Emeralds of the Heart

Emeralds lying by an entrance
unseen, untouched, emeralds of the
heart joining the rise of yearning
past the hour of its bedtime

## Clad High

Clad high in aftermaths stripping tales
from their glare fused in a streak of portioned
alibi scratching time from the ceiling
running the risk of delight rough and
round and ready to move the thread
so often lost in place of safekeeping
sure to lose the day in a hail of blues
that knows what it means
lifting braved stories from the
heart of their meaning

## In Some Ways

the loudest among the human race
are they who are most asleep

## Closing on a Maze

Ashes the weight of rocks in hand

white moans in flecks of sky

bursting in cloned fragility,

guiding waste through capital space,
closing on a maze of still-standings


## Every Life

Every life has its own tones, rhythms, colors; —
harmonizing well with some, not so well
with others

## Alphabets

like notes of a scale joined in endless
combinations — letters turning to words
(to motifs) words to sentences (to melodies)
creating music for the eye as well as the ear

(and also the soul)


## Change but Never Changing

If one doesn't see the paradox of
all things one is not seeing clearly . . .
how in the blink of an eye a world can
change     but the world never changing

## Light

. . . the innocence of life, the vanity
of life, the optimism of life . . .

## Forever Open

Truth . . . sometimes down and out
but always open like a hand
brave to show its wounds and
lines like those of drawn faces
daring an observer to believe in

## The Cutting Edge

... something that must draw blood if it is
to mean something ...

will it be yours?


## Wanting Without

How many want the rain without the thunder
and the sun without the heat

## As the Story Goes

In the all or nothing phase of callings
fixed stances claim their spot like antelopes
struck with dare and asylum
rumored to take the bonds of trust,
tie them in knots and
tug-of-war between themselves
crazy as the story goes

## Caught in a Day's Delight

Caught in a day's delight refusing to let go
refusing to enter the shadow cleared to a head
of close returns nearing the calm of no repeat
promising to be good to her (so good to her),
to sing her to sleep in colors of peace

## Stillness

. . . the black hole of Existence

## By Glass Cages

Scenes by glass cages strict in
camouflage and alibis crossing
funny but deadly deadly but funny
learning much from the serpent and
the snail and the crab running for its
life, not caught on its back
kicking sand in the face of its blessings

## A Coming

of something sweet, of something serious
longing to escape, dying to get out
ready to die if need be    if that
be the price of its song




## Eternal Pregnancy

The spirit in eternal pregnancy . . .
the multiple miracles of joy and terror
lying in womb waiting to be born

## From a Spiritual Shore

A gleam of guided laughter
kindling life in the dark chasms of
soul, blind and freedom-bound
drawing tide from a shore
not yet in the sure of its beginning

## Hands & Knees

Hands raised in prayer unanswered
until they come down . . .
Knees touching the ground with voice
in prayer unanswered
until they rise up . . .

## Before Its Demise

A touch from Love's finger midway
through the story of its surprise
hesitates in its deliverance of
measured cruelties —

A dove's cry blessing the dawn
before its demise

## Life's Song

The Song of Life goes on as the
melodies of lives fade away

## Tools

It's all about tools —
tools to build a self and
keep it in repairs, like
anything else that is raised
and made useful

## Rusting Faithfully

Feeding a rush stuck in counter-ed commotion
rusting faithfully to a spell of Immediacy
and the time that mocks itself filled with
resistance — a binding of the senses to the
insensible floating yeas across the sky
in frames of mined devotion

## Clinging to the Wall of Beat

Of nine plus seven ways to fold a secret
stuff it in the heart and let the bats
play with it, ripping pieces from its body
to bring to their young, blind and sleeping
clinging to the wall of beat    beat    beat

## Always a Place

One always has a place to go, spiritually speaking,
but not always a place of one's choosing

## Going On

Like the prize fighter beaten and fatigued
weary from the battle, not knowing where his
energy is coming from to enable him to go on
still able to move his body and punch, the
artist weary from his battles with Life and Muse
feeling spent, feeling drained but still able to
endure and create, not knowing where his strength
is coming from or how long he'll be able to go on

but he goes on

## A Step or Two

Two children open a door to a stairway
leading to a dark cellar, descending no
further than a couple of steps — one giggles,
turns around and runs back up the stairs —
the other also turns and runs but is frightened,
running back to the safety of the light . . .
This is what most adults do when they take a
step or two into themselves — they quickly
retreat in laughter or fright

## The Noble Aim

. . . to create a self worth being
and worthy of being

## First Wisdom

My life is not about 'me.'

## Two Egos

Two massive egos in conflict with each other
trapped in a room at close quarters —

two scorpions trapped in a jar

## Trouble Spots

Those trouble spots of a life
not always easy to notice or define
like an ink spot on the shirt
the trouble spot beneath the shirt,
beneath the skin — festering wound
that can't be seen can only be felt
*if felt at all* by the one to whom it belongs
and like a tumor or cancerous growth,
the earlier caught the better

## Loser's Revenge

Some let the world have it when it tells them
they just don't have it

## Yes, But

"They said they would help me,
do all they can for me just tell them
what I want, no strings attached."

"Yes, but did they tell you
about the chains . . . "

## Crowded House

The more things you fill your life with
the less space the residents that are already
present have to move around in

## Chipping Away

A man picks and shovels his way through a
wall in his basement laboring in the dim light
so close to dark, working for a breakthrough
to reach something on the other side . . .

This, like the work of one searching for answers
chipping through walls in the depths of his world;
his heart, his mind, his soul


## Abrupt Formations

ceasing to divide, ceasing to form
in reigned transparencies — a
stake too tight for a fit — angles
coming out of sockets, out of
nowhere . . .

a field of eclectic scope
lining shadows cloistered
in a hub of stares
gaining the right of ritual

## Bending a Wave

To be shown a portion of the way
wooing Hope from its den to
bless or scorn in states of trance —
songs of troubadours' hearts
led by miracles standing still
bending a wave of the universe
to the rhythm of their lives


## For the Rose to the Rose

A beam of sunlight cast to the face of a rose
caressed by a morning's wind, the wind then
getting stronger swaying the life of the field in
which the rose stands to a homage of dance
for the rose to the rose, its bud, its thorns,
its place in the heart of Life's soul

## Just a Theory

If there were such a thing as a forensic science
of metaphysics (a contradiction in terms?)
it could prove, by taking spiritual prints of
where we've been on the journey of our past
that wherever we are at any given time in the
process of becoming is precisely where we're
supposed to be and couldn't possibly be
anywhere else (or anyone else) and
what's more, could not have travelled
any other path to get to where we are —

just a theory

## The Object of Objectivity

— to get at the truth of what *is*
in spite of what we are


## In Life's Journey

'Tis wise to think about where you are
going, always . . . but also to *feel* the presence
of where you are, every step of the way

## To Join the Fantasy

Behind the alpha-crave crusted wings
gather in séance — a turban's blue red
spilling the mood (will the angels ever
find their seats) — ushers without
flashlights creeping in the dark
crooked as they go  *the screen
will make you happy  will make
you smile*  will make you proud
in leaving your world behind
to join the fantasy of New Age
reality wrapped in plastic joy

## Truth Colored Glasses

To those with the clearest vision
there is always someone ready to say:
"Excuse me, I think you have something
on your spectacles, a piece of dirt or dust —
here, allow me to clean them for you."

The weakest of the clear-see-ers letting them

## Snake Eyes

A resonance
binding to a
blotted sheath
sacked in
twenty decibels
departing
at the pitch
of dawn —

The day
rolling
snake eyes
for the
heart
of a
storm

## Waiting for the Mind's Sun

On those cloudy days of thought
everything seems black and white,
but everything is still there, is still
*seeable,* waiting for the sun to return
to reveal the true colors of all

# No Forwarding Address

When people move, some travel as near as the house next door; others, the next street; others, across town; others, to the nearest town over; others, to a new city; others to a new state or province; others, to another country; and some (in a metaphysical sense [while still living]) to another world —

no forwarding address

## Pages

breaking from a notebook seeming to detach themselves, freeing themselves from their binders like teeth falling away saying 'adios' as they depart . . . what's it matter? Nothing — unless considering what was written on the pages . . . did *that* have teeth . . .

## To the Artist in Search of a Direction

Think of all you could be doing in the time you spend looking around to see what others are doing . . .

## Not a Guess

From the most pronounced afflictions
to the most subtle — take them away
from a life, *any* life, and that life
would be diminished, would
(in an objective sense) be
worth less —

this a fact, not a guess




## Most Valuable Gems

A back to basics somewhere deep
in the well of Lost Cause searching for
gems of learning, the most valuable to be
found — jewels covered with the muddy
blood of Failure . . . lessons like bees
crowding in a guarded corner protecting
their honey — probing fingers reaching for
the prize     the honey burning like fire

## Sentenced to Life

"I sentence you to life" — (that is, to *life* . . . ).
For most, more frightening are these words
when thought about than the words
    "I sentence you to death"

## Always the Case

One must go further into the invisible dangers
of the unknown, deeper into the dark forests of being
than one has ever gone before to gain even the
smallest increase of enlightenment that lives
beyond the day

## For a Time

In the animal world it's all for a time
about the little ones — brought into being
and cared for above all other needs
but then comes the time when the
babymoon's over, time to get out
and fend for themselves — eat or be
eaten, enter Nature's arena of
Do or Die — the one that they
survived or were protected from,
for a time

## Sometimes Killing

In times of drought the earth is like a
fragile bird dying of thirst, its mouth open
pleading to the sky for the gift that will
sustain it, ready to take all that it can get —

sometimes the sky too generous,
too generous . . . killing in its generosity

## Nature's Ghost

Wind . . . the great ghost of Nature,

constantly moving things

without being seen

## Dream Play

The dream stares without eyes;
its clouded body enveloping the
mind fused to the hour of slumber
moving the play of its phantoms
proud to be host to the entity
that will slay them without mercy
but without malice, deep in the
womb of holy silence

## A World Impervious

Who can tell why the mood has died;
old bracelets turning themselves over for
a piece of the sun . . . trees without hope
refusing to produce a shade for the nth
time this millennium . . . a snake
crawling to shelter not seeming to
mind the ingratitude of a world
shunning its existence
impervious to its crawl
looking for cover behind
the light of cover,
still not knowing what to
do about the apple

## Of Matinees Only

Minds in chains —

spirits in wheelchairs —

bodies as free as the laws of physics
will allow —

criminals protesting the heat and the
cutting of holes stripped of circular grace —

a herd of ordinaries cluttering the streets
beneath the hour mapping Sunday's dress
crucified by silk stalkings

away from the audibles of reprieve
binding raptures to a contract of
matinees only

## As Time Rushes On

Moving commerce by the hour
forever the rush hour —
business heavy on the ground
moving with headshakes and
handshakes shaking the dough
from lives for this junk or that,
as time rushes on

## Of Smile and Frown

A smile says much, oftentimes
more than the frown — but
it also lies more than the frown

## In the Safest Place

. . . that's where art chokes and suffocates —
without dare, without risk . . . banal productions
without teeth    without claw    without fist

## As Far as the Eye Can See

It is on the edge of the cliff where
one can see as far as the eye can see,
out into the horizon and into the abyss

## Somewhere

far off, deep in the spiritual woods
Possibility and Impossibility meet
creating sparks like sticks
rubbing together, like stones
smashing into each other
bringing fire into being

## Lying Bare

A cunning gale halts at the foot of
destruction lying bare its harmonious
dread before a chamber torturous
to all that is impotent; to all that
moves its story to the shores of rebirth
but fails to meet the hour of deliverance

# Beyond Life's Dream

A. I think I want to do it

I think I will do that

I believe I must do that

really believe I need to do it . . .

B. And what is that?

A. To go beyond the dream

## Must It Be

Must everything be a quarrel stripped
to the bone before a truth lies flapping
on the ground like a dying fish
helpless before the sun, pleading
for its release striking in colors
beautiful, perhaps (no doubt)
a clashing of wills wrestling their
energies to see the face of a thing
believed to be hiding itself, yet they
who contend rarely seeing what emerges
with pure objectivity, the thing in
itself telling its story with stoic
genius indifferent to those who
battle in the mud with plastic swords
fighting for the prize of its secret

## Not Yet Ready

Religion — like the four-wheeler of a
child learning to ride a bicycle, one day
removing the safety of the extra wheels . . .
man, in his spiritual development
not yet ready to remove the safety of
religion, to abandon the crutch, still
very much in a beginner's mode,
still (by and large) not yet ready
to grow on his own

## Question

Human Species: "Sincerity, Sincerity . . .
why has thou forsaken me . . . "

Sincerity: "Look to yourself to find the answers
(and all answers to such questions)"

## With Rare Exception

Man . . . his body ever in the present,
his mind musing on the future
or somewhere in the past

## World of Ego

The world of ego is flat —
beyond a certain point, a step
into oblivion

## Of Paying Attention

Many do little with what life delivers
to their attention; a constant stream of
messages and images laid at the entrance
of their minds often lying there like
unopened mail ignored or unnoticed,
mail of the nature that it would
behoove them to open, but it goes
untouched, the occupants home
but not 'home,' occupied
with seeking attention, instead
of paying attention

## Power's Secret

Many things may be done out in the open
yet go unseen, remain unnoticed because
many people don't have their eyes open
(really open) and are rarely open to
suggestions on how to get them open
and once opened, to keep them that way,
open to all that comes before them, open
(especially) to the many forces of the world
that do their best to keep them closed

## A Dangerous Thing

No, I didn't mean that    yes, I said it
but you didn't hear what I said —
yes (no), you didn't *hear* it — No,
(you didn't)    it came out of me right
but went to you wrong . . . .    oh
language can be such a dangerous thing;
can carve a wedge between human beings
at the drop of a word    at the turn of a phrase . . .

## Climbing the Walls (spiritually speaking)

Sometimes this one must do: — must
climb the walls that get to a ceiling that
must be broken through — a ceiling
barring the way to higher levels of
being




## Masked Ball Without the Dance

In any crowded room the perceptive
can see at a glance, that they are present
at a masked ball without the dance

## Life Lite

There are many who have a difficult time
adopting lite in their diets, but not in their lives

## In the Human World

In the human world some sheep are traitors,
leading the wolves to their brothers and sisters —

(and after, often eaten themselves)

## Crossing In and Out

Crossing in and out of one another's path
without a thought, often without a feeling,
people moving on to the next moment of
destiny however significant or futile it may be
and wondering how, only then and now
and only in the minds of a discerning few
how this thing called life can be taken so
lightly by so many, and sometimes also
by the few who do their best to capture a
speck of meaning, grasp it here and there
and express it somehow, somewhere in
some form or other — the least they can do,
they believe, while they live, while they're
here following their path and along the way,
crossing in and out of the paths of others
in various states of awareness

## An Artist Must Stay on His Toes . . .

not done by staying in bed watching TV
eating foods of pizza and chocolates
and ice cream being served by lovers
pausing only to clip the nails of one's toes


## Not Always on Time

Emotions exploding in the heart
fragments rising to the mind
delivered to the page just in time

(not always on time . . . )

## Solitary Line

A line hangs alone    all alone;
nothing near it or close to it, leading a
solitary existence then one day it's
needed, called into service, asked to
give up its autonomy for a greater good —
(Don't worry, we'll take care of you;
you'll like your new home — we
promise — ) and off it goes,
taken away by a page of words to
become part of a literary family

## To a Suicide Friend

You left us because you failed to
put your life in its proper order
when there's no such thing as a
proper order to life —

Life could have told you that

## Poems

The best poems are the poems
that write themselves, or at least
give up their skeletons; leaving
the poet to add their flesh . . .

his blood

## Solitude Shared by Two

To adjoining corridors one moves
quietly, stepping toward spaces solitary
yet connected one to the other
passing through each other steady
in their silence, teaching the stoic
beauty of a solitude shared by two

## Between Eyes

Oh the conversations between eyes
(the right pairs of eyes) — putting the
tongue to shame, piercing into the world
of mind, into the universe of the soul
exchanging thoughts and feelings
beyond what words can say

## With and Without

There is suffering in both heaven and hell
(i.e. the heaven and hell on earth).
The former is suffering that births vision
and insight, the latter is suffering that doesn't

## The Highest Love

. . . i.e. love beyond the passions . . .
the highest spiritual love — like Fire
burning in fire, steady in its power . . .
few hearts brave enough to receive it,
fewer strong enough to bring it forth

## Truth at All Cost

... yes — but oh what it costs
to live by this sentiment

## By Grace to Dust

To the ends of harbored states by grace to
dust invertible, the mantel cool as ceilings
dampened by an autumn rain ... glass
implodes in the mirror grievous as a
prisoner's assault, dividing tales of love
broken as a two-step turning for a
break of light, a halting of rest,
a summons to life

## Place of Heed

Motioned to a place of heed . . .
whole byways cross entwined like
closing fingers of strangers
touching for the first time
stepping high into the promise of
tomorrow, veiling the path that leads
to hope paved with ways of sorrow

## Paradox Indispensable

Billions of years, all elements of existence
working together yet against each other
groove to groove, blade to blade,
moving the ship of Life

## More Slowly in the Depths

Thoughts as swift as lightning on the surface —
yes — many thoughts moving on the surface . . .
but like movement under water or through
deep sand or snow, things move more slowly
in the depths

## The Way of Good Fortune

The sun is always shining, yet not
shining at any time on every one,
but always shining on some —

and so too the way of good fortune


## Sometimes Better from the Shore

Sometimes the best fishing is from the shore . . .

(a word to the spirit-venturer setting his sail
for spiritual treasure)

## On a Rising

Where the waters speak of saviors
turning toward the sun, and mists of
light etch sacreds on an ocean sky,
and waves undaunted wade a
riddle's watch, winged in starlit
nights crossing currents of dew
untouched by blessing's might,
and passions abide fading to
clear awash in dreams dividing,
alliance bows to something graced
born on the rising of a wind song
raised on climbs of ecstasy
touching the heart of vision's way
through pours of jagged peace,
powering the wild of free

## Always Speaking

Nature is always speaking to us

without our knowing it —

without its knowing it —



## Of Newborn Life

The fragility of newborn life, all life —
from the tiger to the swan . . . awesome
in its frailness, to what it shall become

## A Child's Exploration

Bending down to see
the face in the flower
the flower looking up
to see the flower
in the face

## Never More Giving

Icicles decorating every tree, clinging to
every branch in sight looking like silver
shining in the sun, the air not yet warm
enough to melt . . . the snow-covered grounds
adding to the scenery as magnificent as
one could ever see, everything beaming
with the cool of winter's spirit, now
calm and beautiful in its simplicity . . .
Nature never more giving to the eyes,
the soul, the heart

## On Standing the Heat

Even for the best pair of lungs it's hard
to get a good breath of air when the
temperature is 98° and the dew point 75
(the stifling air) . . . as close to unbearable
as it could be — a metaphor here . . .
something to do with the spiritual —
something about standing the heat,
taking it, though it can beat up on the
strongest and bravest among us

## Doing What They Must

The grandest spirits do not look for happiness —
they go about their business doing what they
must do, giving it their best, and sometimes
happiness comes to them, sometimes unex-
pectedly, something joyous from out of the
blue giving them pleasure, at times for only
a moment, and for a moment taking pause
reflecting on the gift they've received along
their way then back to the work at hand
doing what needs to be done, giving their task
the best of themselves and in so doing
creating a happiness not always felt
but somehow always with them, like a
rainbow not always seen but always
present, glowing warmly above

## Up to You

Your life wakes anew each day,
but it is up to you to embrace
its new offerings, or stay by
the grave of your yesterdays

## The Poet's Business

A taking in of all there is,
this not possible, never to be done
yet still the poet's business . . .

to seek     to reach     to find

# Part Two

# First Page

I touch the first page of a pad, a virgin pad,
touched with my pen . . . I will try to be
good to you, I will try to be gentle;
but when passion comes I make no
promises; then it is up to the words . . .
they will speak as they will, saying
what they have to say . . . I hope they
will not hurt you, and the stroke of my
pen will not draw too much blood

# A Field

like an ocean of earth, the wind
bending its life like ripples of waves,
the dirt road on which one stands,
like a beach of dark sand beneath
the sky overhead, the same sky
that blankets the waters and
accommodates life blessed with
wings that land on both bodies
of the world with peace in the
field of space and time

## Ephemeral Portrait

A drizzle two chills from a muddy Sunday
carved a portrait of moment-to-moment
on the gray of a sky face down, eyes up,
appealed by strict improvisation . . .
The sun lighting the canvas
(for a moment) breaking
before the clouds


## A Toss of Reverence

Gales crossing the bridge in broad
behavior crossing from left to right
lifting the ocean's blood to the
employment of baptism, hailing
the structure man has so proudly built . . .
I stand in awe of their power
and toss my reverence to the wind

# In Metaplay Only

In gallant seasoning a meaning
primed to perfection coveting branches
whose leaves have blown away but for
one floating gently to the ground in
ballet motion, escaping the will of
the wind descending in its own time
at its own pace, defying all laws of gravity
with finesse of style and grace —

in metaplay only

## Places Privileged

Half-moon holding its own in the
midnight sky inspiring tales through
the ages — its better half hiding in the
dark like a child hiding in a closet
learning early the pleasures of the
secret world hidden from all eyes
the silence on the walls entering into
places privileged, the world outside
tangled in a web of insensibles
with no one there to free them

## Holding a Balance

Of knowledge crushing possibilities
unheard of, not thought of — the mystery
of one — two — three measuring its reach
to the nearest particles of mind
circling the future of a past
to take for its share the duty of
angels holding the balance from
fading to falling between
one to none and all

## Wound Up

I set my mind to grasp at
straws for a while and wound up
with a cerebral cocktail of fire

## A Mutt Called Freedom

The morning cursed, thirsty and blind;
rumors brought to the attention of a scene
chained to a mutt called Freedom jumping for
its daily crumbs, the soft voice of a child
calling through a nearby house — the doors
locked, the rooms empty — the windows
open wide, all too high for the little one
to reach — to witness Freedom jumping
for its crumbs, panting before the dawn

## How Much Is Seen

Everything comes with the morning,
yet man sees only 0.000000001%
of all there is . . .

(if this)


## Lives

. . . like dreams fading slowly
(ever so slowly)

day      after day      after day

after day      by day      after

day      into night

## Reaching Boldly

Reaching boldly into the mouth of Glory
does man do, Glory taking off less than
it can devour, man taking hold of more
than he can chew

## Political Battles

. . . what more than deciding the outcome
of which illusions shall rule the day —
Reality somewhere picnicking,
somewhere far away

## Poets & Madmen

Jeering the parade of life as it passes,
scolding it, taunting it, telling the marchers
they're out of step, they've got it all wrong . . .
their costumes and uniforms, the direction
they are going, and the music played badly
(so badly) beating from behind

## What Can He Tell Us

The man in suit and tie . . .

can he be telling us anything but lies?

And even if he speaks his truth, born

out of the establishment from which

he is entrenched . . .

Is this truth not also     a lie . . . ?

## May It Be Asked

To those looking over the children's shoulders
watching what they do, what it is they are up to . . .

Who (may it be asked) is watching over you

## Sunday Then Monday

How many pray to God on Sunday
then dance around the calf of gold
on Monday

## Not Ringing True

A schoolboy cutting his losses, tossing his marbles
in the dirt, snapping his crayons bleeding their
color in his hands before being taken to a
basket of waste joined by pens and pencils,
deciding all is just a waste of time, and
time itself perhaps a waste, and life too
as he's coming to know it, leaving his books
by a cement wall where pigeons gather
to coo and leave their droppings, a
boy invaded by a storm of questioning
sensing for the first time that most of what he's
been told is false, just doesn't ring true, the lies
all picture-blue . . . in the background
the final school bell ringing

## In the Details Only

Strange how most people live only
in the details of their lives, or the
single words of its story . . .
never experiencing the whole,
never living the full journey

## How Many Missed

How many lives we have missed by doing
that instead of this — every movement,
thought, gesture, destroying a thousand
possibilities, a thousand possible lives
that will never be because it is *that*
movement, *that* thought, *that* gesture
and no other which influences everything
that follows till the final breath of life . . .

how many lives must be missed
(in every moment of a life)

## Paradox

In the apparent, i.e. on its surface, life
reveals no meaning, has no purpose,
yet a human being must, if he or she
is to be worthy of life's gift, have or
create meaning and purpose

## Reminder

The sand that slips between my fingers
reminds me of the death of all things

## In Offering

The night was cool, yet calm, ready for her
offering . . . the gray life shedding its sorrow
preparing to dance, and dance she did . . .
free of woe, the song of her being filling the
air, the crowd around her unaware of her,
moving to their own joy for some joyous
occasion, but from this crowd she stood out,
coming out of her wounds touching the hand
of grace telling her that this was her moment,
that all for now was right . . . a coming of
day in the winter of a life celebrated with
the confidence of spring, lifting her spirit
in offering to Life's Spirit, filled with love
and gratitude for her journey in spite of . . .
because of . . . thanking the gods for this time
and for her life, kissing the world goodnight

## Within Pain

There is a place within pain where it
becomes so intense that it produces
the most peaceful calm, even bliss,
yet with an immense feeling of
knowing, truly knowing
what it means to be    *alive*



## What Remains

Imagine everything falling away from
your life except that which cannot fall —
what remains is the core of your being,
the essence of your life

## Should Always Be One

No matter what you do it will never
be enough for some people, their
'never enoughness' born of ignobility
and pettiness — but there should be
one person for whom it will never
be enough for reasons that are noble,
that person being you

## Even in Paradise

Even in paradise one must cultivate
one's own garden

## Of the Genius of Nature

No force of Nature knows what the other
forces are doing, but how beautifully
they complement one another

# Fills with Wonder

How the sky fills the mind with wonder
when lying on the grass looking up
at the night doing the impossible
of counting the distant stars or
staring down the sun in the dark

## Realized in a Moment

Realized in a moment of peace
an escaping thought circles the air
above the calm, stern in its laughter
yet without scorn, drawing a breath
of freedom from the space of silence
longing to disturb the stillness of itself

## Time

. . . the only thing that everyone is
brave enough or fool enough to kill

## What Death and the Highest Things in Life Have in Common . . .

they both take one's breath away

## A Cool Start

'Tis a cold parent, Winter, as cold as
the dead, to the warm child Spring,
that gets off to a cool start

## Found Mentor

An old sage whose life was nearing its end
took a young student in his care into a
village to find him a new mentor. There he
encountered a gathering of people in lively
conversation but for one sitting alone with
his thoughts. The sage politely introduced
himself and proceeded to ask them a variety
of questions, every member of the gathering
having an answer for each one, save for the
man sitting alone who answered all questions
with the words "I don't know." At the end
of the questioning, the sage turned to the
boy and smiled, saying that he had found
among this group a good mentor for him,
the wisest among them, which was the
man sitting alone answering all questions
with, "I don't know."

## Like a Great Athlete Never Used

The mind . . . its potential like a great athlete
never used, always sitting on the bench,
his gifts gone unnoticed, his powers such
that he could win the game if allowed to,
if only given the chance; but he just sits
patiently on the bench waiting to be used,
waiting to show what he can do

# Bending but Not Yielding

How grand the shrub appears holding its ground
standing against the river, its powerful flow
split, disrupted, taking everything with it in
the path of its current except a few great
rocks, their dark gray backs like mounds
exalted, raised above the water, and the
little shrub bending but not yielding,
standing tall against the mighty river
unable to defeat it, to bring it down,
forced to flow around it

## Grand Enough

There are spirits grand enough that they can
reach out and give the world a hug —

(some of them misanthropes)


## Never to Be Known

It may be that no human being could survive
for a second in the skin (i.e. the world)
of another human being —

this never to be known

## Lost Promise

A sudden ache, a trembling of
washed hands, a shudder two
paces from a heart in short desire
to rest in wounds unhealing,
fulfilling a promise made to love
so very long ago

## Not for Everyone

Stories hidden between pages papered in
song heard only by the deaf, seen only by
the blind in rows of warrants fading,
turning toward defiance as toward a sun
revealing itself as enemy through hearts
severed deep in scenes of ballad-play
not rising for all . . . set not
for everyone

## Preservation

Preserving the aisle of wreckage rich with
pollinized dread and boarding rooms free of
rats and hazing sworn luxuriant basking in
a golden shade guarding a language simple
in its aim from a millennium unfolding in
vermillion pace through maelstroms of
Sinceria and the stars' perfect chaos
probing inventions of a distant dark
knowing nothing of runaway shame
or the measure of ancient needs
burning with intensity

## Cover of Surprise

Where amber falls as quiet as leaves
covering the ground of their descent
a wall stands courteous inviting a
reach over itself with bodies of
liquid space moving in earnest to
the nameless tying their world to a
cloud of triggered ends betting
heavily on the folding of armed
fingers and decoys of painted
soldiers tasting the power of a glance
stored in the barracks of a sky
binding hope to a cover of surprise
halting a journey's start

## In Vision

A man sitting in a chair, the chair
slowly disappearing from beneath him
he's writing on a table also disappearing
the man soon sitting and writing in the air
also disappearing

only pen and paper remain now floating away
taking his words with them

## Imprisoned Fantasies

Imprisoned fantasies longing to be
present for Reality's Parade to cheer and
cast roses as it passes — unable to be there . . .
Reality, the more disappointed of the
two . . . for without them, Reality is lost —
knows that it cannot be . . .
cannot do . . .

## No One Noticed

It was time to go    nobody knew what
that meant, all hanging around in their lives
without a thought to think watching a white handkerchief
blowing close by on a path that no one noticed before,
something to do with surrender    but nobody
noticed the hint; the sky then began to cloud,
but no one noticed    thunder rumbled in the
distance, no one seemed to change or notice —
a universe was running out of time, the future
breathing heavily of fear    no one cared to notice

## To the Dogs

Gone to the dogs — yes, that's where he's gone
the bum on Angel Road seen crawling this
morning down on his face by a sign standing tall
on the side of the road — cars roared by
not one bothering to stop, too much hurt,
too much disgust to subject themselves to,
the drivers operating on the conviction that
everyone deserves what he gets, eventually
gets what he deserves — the hounds of Cavalry
following close behind

# Fault Lines

Fault lines fractured, running through
condition-human like veins through a body
diseased, about to burst — the forever-drive
toward greater bounty — whatever's in one's
best interest — (yes! we'll call this virtue! I've
got mine so go get yours, unless I wake tomorrow
and decide I want more, that I want yours).
We'll build our lives our temples on hills
that stand above — ignore the tremors and
rumblings from below where the waste of
all we do to get where we are accumulates,
destroying, destroying, crumbling the foundation
of dignity and the ground on which we stand
lifting our glasses in toast to ourselves
the ground preparing a place of fire to
smash them

## 10, 20, 30% Off . . .

10, 20, 30% off . . .
to be found in commerce, always . . .
but also in the buying and selling
of souls

## Comfort Killers

They say it's not the fire that kills
most of the time, but the smoke —
and what is smoke but the essence
of what the fire burns? And much of
the furniture and appliances of the
modern home, made of plastics and
other materials toxic and deadly when
met with flames . . . yes, comforts of the
modern household . . . killers they are,
in more ways than one

## Bourgeois Paranoia

"Whatever happens, keep smiling,
and don't speak unless spoken to.
Your life may be at stake."

"But I'm only applying for a job."

"Precisely."

## Balloons in the Air

Children hitting a balloon in the air
filled with air, keeping it in the air . . . the
so-called movers and shakers of the world
doing no more — simply putting their
spin on things, and in the long run
accomplishing what more than that of
children hitting their balloons in the air

# Pressing Buttons

. . . like putting money in a jukebox . . .
selecting keys with letters and numbers,
knowing exactly what music will be played
by pressing them . . . people too, more than a
few can be played the same way — pressing
their buttons, selected keys, knowing what songs
they will sing or play for you, and in what way

## Wanting

Of those who want *things*, many things . . .
so many wanting in many things . . .
their hearts tied to an anchor that wants
to hold as well as float, leaving them
wanting     wanting . . . the fog
of their lives drifting without a horn

## Modern Deficit

Lawnmower — as loud as can be . . . its rider
oblivious to the thoughts it is chasing away,
not allowing to come into being — and
another in the close distance, and others
on nearby streets noising loudly the air;
and weed cutters, and hedge trimmers
and a thousand other machines always
active somewhere, always, keeping ideas
from manifesting that may have value,
have meaning . . . lost to the age and
world, compliments of noisy, often
polluting machines now ever in operation
(the cost for mowing a lawn or the like,
sometimes something beyond measure)

## Walking in Their Sleep

Between Sensitivity and Insensitivity
moves a line of middle-of-the-roaders
farther than the mind's eye can see
feeling no heat from one side or the
other side, walking in their sleep

## Easy Entry

People every day break into other people's
lives — among the easiest locks to pick . . .
they look around and help themselves to
whatever's around that they may help
themselves to . . . their easiest targets
(like that of all burglars), the places
(the people) where there's nobody home

# What Price

What it costs the violinist to play the notes
of the violin, to bring forth beauty through
fingertips once soft and now calloused
from years of toil and practice
pressing strings to neck (steel to wood)
with fingers that once ached, and also
heart to make the music sing . . .

pain, the price for this beauty, and
all human-created beauty there is

## How Many Swamplands

How many swamplands must one
wade through in one's soul to get to its
highlands, its flowing rivers, its mighty sea (!) . . .

## Like Rare Flowers

The rarest minds and spirits . . .
some found in places where they're not
supposed to be; like rare flowers found
where they're not supposed to grow,
not expected to be

# My Oh My

*"It's not there — just doesn't exist;
nothing of the world is greater than I!"*

Oh the capacity of most humans to ignore
what is beyond them, to block out what is
too strong for their minds to handle, too
painful for their hearts to face . . . greatness
that quakes the soul as far removed
from their senses as stars in the distance
hiding from the daylight . . .

*"Nothing of the world is greater than I!"*

my oh my

## Never Without Beauty

Going for it — for something beyond — a
journey to something greater than oneself . . .
not without risk (no, never without risk);
doesn't always work out — sometimes
disastrous, sometimes the loss of life . . .
but you take what courage and ability
the powers that be have given you and
go for it — sometimes being shot down
at great heights or self-destructing in
mid-flight as tragedy strikes —
(yes, sometimes it strikes . . . );
but if the journey is brave and true
the tragedy is not without beauty
and can be, to the eyes willing to see,
oh so beautiful

## More Vast Than the Distance Between the Stars

Loneliness works its miracles on one nature, its curses on another, separated only by the gifts of their silence . . . by a distance more vast than the distance between the stars

## Amidst the Gray Shadow

Amidst the gray shadow of all that is not lies the reflection of all that will be

## Life Needs Its Prayer

. . . its vintage promise to lay
in the lap of the dead

## Images

swirling about in a circle of dreams;
skies moving slowly so as not
to disturb them . . .

a shiver greets the dawn moved
in guiled sentiment releasing its
truth to a world that will not hold

## Perhaps

Perhaps God is a lost child
waiting for man to find Him

## Dream of a Dream

Birds — so many birds filling the sky
coming from all directions, each carrying
a piece of Thought born unto a dream
inside the Dream of the Cosmos

## A Twilight

napping in the crest of a moon
years beyond the waves it will rise
shimmering in the mind of Shiva
still sleeping in his wedding gown
his sons out hunting snakes in
Time's garden coveting The Way
carving cynicals above the rule of
waiting, gaining its order through
signs of remembrance and all
crowned goals of here-to-stay

## One Day Open

A sigh crucial to a morning's glance
in ribbons red wrapping the hour for a
time not setting in place . . . but Beauty
takes it all, takes it so rapturedly to a
marsh of fallen rainbows clutching
the rays of a sun in her hand she'll
one day open releasing a butterfly to
claim the world

## To the Edge

By an evening's cross filled with ancient
promise spaces behind thoughts stripped

like felons lying in a drum only the eyed
can see — scores of yellowed strife lordly

moved to a fate reconstructed holding in
countdowns and scales of crystal might

pushing changes to the edge of a stage
for a turning of blue mourning

breaking before light

## Stirred to Life

A fire-spiritual burning around the pit
of emptiness stirring the dead to life —
sleeping shadows of inner-being lying
at the base of dimensions raising a sigh
to the flame warming the pathway to
miracles soon to be born . . . to
treasures of soul yearning to be

## Whole in Peace

Of days parallel conditioned to hold by stake
the hour's magic emerging whole in peace
revealing one can live without masters,
can thrive without false tales and ways of
old, can draw near to every wrong without
falling into an abyss, move with courage
before obstacles forever rising, feeding the
darkness with bits of light, questioning
every right

## Covered Ground

Coy in his desert heart a monk with
cautioned feet covers the ground
stepped by the faithful examining
closely the maps of those who
refused to follow

## Cost What It May

The artist working to the ends of his
bravery must ultimately stick his head
into the lion's mouth, cost him what it may

## More in Common Than This

Poet and spider . . . one weaves his poems
while the other weaves his web . . . and
more have they in common than this

## What Sometimes Happens

An artist going to a source of inspiration
again and again, always being good to him
always giving him something for his time
and sometimes trouble then one day
he goes to it and it doesn't give anymore,
the giving gone without warning like a
familiar store open one day and closed
the next, everyone and everything
connected with it vanishing without a trace

## Song That Won't Be Sung

Movement following tracks covered almost
complete — the doe rounding back, searching
for her fawn lost in the bolting of the herd
and the riddle of a hunter's scope
the woods lost within themselves whispering
of murder in the snow, the blood-remains
still warm yet swallowed by the cold . . .
a mother lifting her ears to hear the call
of her young     listening intently
for the song that won't be sung

## Rare the Life

Rare is the life that doesn't have
clouds that return now and again,
blocking the sun of its day

## Tears and Pain

. . . the first guests to arrive at
your birth, the last to leave your grave

## Everywhere the Heart Goes

We leave a piece of ourselves behind
everywhere our hearts go, and in turn
take things away with us, much
which we don't know

## Meaning

We are told that "this is a tree," "this is
a flower," "this is a bird," this a rock,
this a blade of grass . . . but these things
cannot have meaning or become a
reality for us until we ask ourselves:
"what is a tree? what is a flower?
a bird, a rock, a blade of grass . . ."

## Can See Magic

Children can see magic all around them; especially the ones who, with a little time and experience, can turn the commonplace into scenes of magic

## Serenity of Love

. . . like a lioness contented
stretching her paws in the
morning sun

## Your Way

You     are the way to your world

## Thoughts

tapping on one's mind . . .
as joyous and comforting as
taps on the shoulder by a
loved one, not seen for
some time

## Words of the Soul — To the Soul

Some cool          some warm
some hot           some cold
some sipped      some gulped
some sweet       some tart
some cutting strings    some making strings
some revealing    some concealing
some moving on   some moving out
some wooing      some shooing

all playing their part in the process
of healing and growing

## No Greater Benefit

Early to grow, early to see,

early to know, early to be,

i.e. to become . . . to be free

. . . no greater benefit can a
human being have than this

## Every Moment of One's Life

Every moment of a life never to repeat
never to be again, flowing one into the next
in simultaneous birth and death, flowing
without pause, without rest . . . how
grand, how priceless the once-in-a-lifetime
fragments of time that make up a life
also never to be repeated. Is this not
cause for wonderment, every moment
of one's life

## Keeping On

To keep going, keep doing, keep
questioning, keep creating, keep loving,
keep growing, keep trying to be the best
that you can be is to win the honor of
leaving the world with the knowledge
you've done your best; that you've
earned the right to exit your life
with dignity, blessing and peace

## Who Lift Their Eyes

Those who lift their eyes above the
necessities to sustain their existence
seeing more, requiring more, thirsting
for more, reaching for *life* pulsing
on the spiritual vine waiting for minds
and hearts to receive its offerings,
paying the price as their spirits
sing to the top of their voice
through loves and pains and joys,
the music of those who lifted their
eyes beyond themselves and
reached for Life's Eternal.

ABOUT THE AUTHOR

Carroll Blair is an award-winning author of more than twenty books. His work has been well endorsed and commendably reviewed, as illustrated by the following commentary from Midwest Review, which proclaimed, "The poetic expression of Carroll Blair is both unique and compelling. Using word images like the strokes of a painter's brush, Blair creates a resonating recognition that is the mark of a master poet."
He is an alumnus of the Boston Conservatory and lives in Massachusetts.

www.ingramcontent.com/pod-product-compliance
Lightning Source LLC
Chambersburg PA
CBHW032359040426
42451CB00006B/59